ZEN FILMMAKING
THE MANIFESTO

SCOTT SHAW

Buddha Rose Publications

Zen Filmmaking: The Manifesto
Copyright © 1997 By Scott Shaw
www.scottshaw.com
www.zenfilmmaking.com

All Rights Reserved.

No Part of this book may be reproduced in any manner without the expressed written permission of the author or the publishing company.

Zen Filmmaking is a Registered Trademark.

First Edition 1997

ISBN 10: 1-949251-05-5
ISBN 13: 978-1-949251-05-0

Library of Congress:
69427833323

Printed in the United States of America

10 9 8 7 6 5 4 3 2 1

Zen Filmmaking
The Manifesto

Zen Filmmaking: The Manifesto

Fade In:

I created *Zen Filmmaking* in 1991 as a way to make the filmmaking process as easy, as creative, and as pain free as possible. To do that, at the heart of *Zen Filmmaking* is the fact that a Zen Filmmaker does not use a script or a screenplay in the creation of a film.

The Screenplay

Many people base all of their filmmaking creativity around a screenplay and they question, *"How can you create a movie without a screenplay?"*

To answer, the reality of it is; in your mind's eye, you can write a great script. And, in that script, you have great locations, great sets, and your actors act out every word perfectly. But, the truth of independent filmmaking is, it is usually not like that.

First of all, as an independent filmmaker, you commonly do not have the money to get the locations and/or the sets that you have detailed in your screenplay. This is particularly the case if you have written an elaborate script. But, more importantly, it is quite common that due to the fact you will mostly likely be working with novice actors, they will not possess the developed ability to memorize dialogue and then speak those lines with any convincing realism. This is the reason that a large percentage of independent films are seen as unprofessional—the actors portraying their characters come off as unreal.

But now, think about this… If you have a story in mind, and I am not saying don't have a story. Because when I create a movie, I always have a story in mind. But, once you have that general storyline, instead of writing an elaborate screenplay; simply put together a cast that can bring out the essence of the characters you have in mind for your movie, and then move forward and create that film.

Casting

One of the main, and most essential points of *Zen Filmmaking* to remember is, *"Your cast does not have to be professionally trained actors"* As they will not be required to memorize dialogue, (and then recite those written words with conviction), all you have to do is to gather a group of people together who look the way you want your characters to look and who can portray the emotions of the characters you have in mind for your story in the most natural manner possible.

By creating your movie with this as a basis, once you have your story, and have put together your cast, you can simply go out and find one or more locations, bring your cast to the set, and shoot your movie. It's as simple as that!

No rehearsals. Just filmmaking in its purest sense.

The Cast

I am often asked about how to best acquire a cast for a Zen Film. The main thing about casting your Zen Film is to remember, *"Some actors get it—they intrinsically understand the process of Spontaneous Creativity, and some do not."*

Most true actors actually want to *improv*. Why? Because by improving they get to add their own creative signature to the film.

Then, there are the ones who don't get it—the actors who must have a script. Those are the people who are really locked into different era and style of filmmaking. They want things to be fed to them. They don't want to be naturally creative.

Many people have asked me, *"What do you do with an actor or an actress who is resistant on the set?"*

To answer, *"I don't use 'em!"*

In short, find actors who are open minded to this style of natural, spontaneous creativity. If they become resistant on your set, simply ask them to leave.

As previous stated, you don't have to use professional actors!

In terms of my filmmaking, many times I'll meet a person and they have a really interesting look or possess a very interesting personality. From this alone, I bring them on a movie and put them in the film.

…Because they don't have to memorize dialogue, they don't have to be locked into a character—they can simply be themselves. And, as stated, from this, the overall presentation of the movie, (to the audience), is much more natural.

The Crew

This, *"Naturalness,"* is the same ideology I use with my crew. You want to surround yourself with people who are creative, can think on their feet, and are not dominate by structure. You need people who are willing to change their minds at a moment's notice.

Just as with the true actor, true cinematographers and true filmmakers are always open to change and make themselves available and open to new and different inspiration.

In defining whom you should work with, the best thing to do is to meet with your crew and discuss this philosophy before you actually get out there in the trenches and are filming. Because, the fact of the matter is, you want to know that your crew is going to stand behind you once your production is in motion.

Guiding the Actor

The question is also often asked, *"If I don't use a script, how do I get my story told?"*

First of all… One of the primary understandings of *Zen Filmmaking* is, *"The stories have all been told."* If you think the story in your movie is totally original, you are lying to yourself. With this as the elemental basis, to answer the question, what I do is I get my actors on the set, I tell them what the scene is about, and I describe to them the essence of what I want them to portray or discuss in that scene. Then, I let them go at it. Many times, that is all the guidance they need and they develop the storyline with their own unique flavor.

If, on the other hand, they need any tuning-up about the story development, I stop the scene and guide them in the direction I want the story to go. Then, I recommence shooting.

Ultimately, what happens by letting an actor be themselves is that you get a very-very natural performance. Two people, three people, four people, or however many people are in the scene, you let them talk the way they talk, and develop their characters the way they develop their characters. From this, you get a very natural performance that is then presented to your audience.

Critiquing

A lot of people want to criticize independent features; whether they're *No-Budget, Low-Budget, B-Movies, Cult Films, Zen Films,* or whatever... But, like I always say, *"What is a film critic? With very few exceptions, a film critic is somebody who doesn't have the talent or the dedication to actually go out and make a movie."*

Because, let's face facts... Making a movie is not easy. Even with *Zen Filmmaking,* it takes a lot of focus and creative energy.

As far as the critics go, it's easy for someone to sit around and criticize films. I mean, even in the highest budget films, you can find flaws, and you can find things to criticize.

Criticizing filmmaking is very easy. But, to actually make a movie, is not easy! In fact, it's very complicated. Which again is where *Zen Filmmaking* comes into play and one of the primary reasons I created it.

Zen Filmmaking is about removing as many obstacles as possible from the filmmaking process.

Make the Mistakes Your Friend

It is essential to note, *"Obstacles,"* are the primary reason many would-be filmmakers want to start a film but never do. This is also the reason many filmmakers start to create a movie but do not complete it.

Many people start a film. But, as anybody who has ever begun walking down the road to a film's creation knows, *"There will be problems!"* In fact, every movie I've ever made, (and I've made a lot of 'em), there have been problems that have occurred with every single one of them. Some have been small. Some have been big. But, no film is every created without encountering some level of problems.

The fact of the matter is, you will never be able to create a movie without encountering some level of obstacles. There are going to be problems. But, *Zen Filmmaking* teaches that what you need to do is to make those obstacles part of your creative process. Like I always say, *"Make the mistakes your friend."* Because, if you, *"Make the mistakes your friend,"* then you can work within those parameters and make them part of your overall creative process.

This gets us back to the topic of other people criticizing films and, in fact, you, criticizing your own movie…

You must remember that no movie is every going to turn out exactly the way you want it to turn out. For example, as an artist, I've painted for most of my life. And, I can tell you; no painting ever turns out exactly the way I had planned.

What you need to do, regarding the filmmaking process is, you need to understand that you have to allow a movie to be what it is. Let it be, within itself.

We all want any film we make to look a certain way and to turn out a certain way. As such, we work towards that end. That's fine. But, you cannot allow what you hope something will be, to define your movie. Things are going to happen that you are not going to like. And, if you hope to actually complete your film, instead of shutting it down and throwing in the towel during production, you have to learn to accept and live within that understanding.

Use What's Available

This brings us back to the point of, *"Make the mistakes your friend."*

With the dawning of creative and artistic movie making everything changed. Certainly, in the 1950's and 1960's, the realms of filmmaking were definitely pushed forward into the areas of the artistic and the abstract. But, I believe it was more exemplified with the dawning of the age of music videos.

What happened was, with the birth of artistic filmmaking, (and music videos are just that), there came to be a new and expanded understanding that a film can be as abstract as you want it to be. Colors can be anything. Scenes can be anything. Your cuts can be as erratic as you desire them to be. So, instead of becoming upset with your project if you find unexpected flaws, make all of that a part of your filmmaking process and use it as an actual signature for the film you are creating.

Certainly, you try to get a scene looking the way you want it to look. But, if it doesn't happen, allow yourself to be free and creative enough to be able to use the elements and the things that are available to us now in order to complete your film.

Early in the Game

When I first began making films, we were shooting on actual film and it was very-very expensive. You had to buy the film. You had to develop the film. Then, you had to make copies of the film so you could edit the movie. This was done because you did not want to damage your original footage. So, you either copied the film to a work-print or you transferred the film to video with timecode where it was then edited on *Three Quarter Inch Masters* or *Beta Masters*. Then, after you completed the edit, you would Telecine the film to correct minor color or lighting imperfections. This process, at its cheapest, cost one-hundred dollars an hour.

With *Telecine* you could somewhat change the overall look of the film. If it was a little dark, you could bring up the light. If it was little light, you could bring it down. And, you could change the overall color texture of the film to a certain degree. But, for the most part, you were left with what you had shot.

Today, you can do all of these lighting and color correction and more on your computer. But, even with this ability, your film is probably not going to be the exact way you may have envisioned it to be. Your D.P. may have shot certain scenes a little dark. He, (or she), may have shot them a little light. The scenes may be out of focus. Or, there may be some audio problems. But, these factors should not be a reason to stop you or stop the film!

What I am saying is to take all of those elements: out of focus, poor lighting, color variations, whatever, make them a part of your creative, finished product.

If you have to add coloration to your film or if you have to make it black and white instead of color, do it! Use all of the things at your disposal to get your finished product out there!

That is the ultimate lesson of *Zen Filmmaking*. Make a movie and get it out there!

Make the Process Happen

In short, in *Zen Filmmaking,* what you do is to start out with a story. Then, you go out there and film it. When you look at your competed footage, if it's not quite what you expected, that's fine. It's all part of the process.

From making a movie in this manner you can learn while you get a new film out there. Then, in your next movie, you will understand, *"Well... I made a little miscalculation doing that on my last film, so I won't do it again. I didn't like what happened when I did that, so I'm going to do it a different way this time."*

From all of these experiences, the next time you make a film, it will be so much better. And that's the ultimate thing about filmmaking—doing it, completing a project, and getting it out there as a calling-card. Getting it out there to entertain the masses.

Removing the Obstacles

As stated, the main thing about *Zen Filmmaking* is that it's about removing as many obstacles as possible from the filmmaking process. It's about being as spontaneous as possible.

What that means is that you don't want to lock yourself into a highly defined mindset—full of preconceived definitions. You want to leave your mind open so that you can adapt to new creative ideas and experiences when they present themselves to you.

For example, when I go out and shoot a movie, I have my cast and I have some ideas of where I am going to shoot. But, if I see a new location while driving and think, *"Wow, this would really work in the film,"* we get out of the car and we go and do one or more scenes at the location.

And, the fact of the matter is, you never know what's going to happen. This is why in *Zen Filmmaking* we don't use scripts. Because with no script, you are allowed to be free in your own, *"Spontaneous Creation."* So, if I see a location, my cast and crew are allowed to go there and film. That's where the magic of *Zen Filmmaking* happens. You don't lock yourself into a structured process.

Structure

For the filmmakers who still desire some form and structure in the filmmaking process, I can tell them what I do while creating one of my Zen Films. First, I have a shot list. Each day, I create a shot list of the scenes I want to have happen for the movie. Then, I allow freedom and the magic of Zen to take over. So, if we are driving along, we see a location, we get out, and we'll film a scene or two. Maybe it works, maybe it doesn't. But, what I come away with is at least a few more minutes of footage that will add to the overall production value of the film.

In independent filmmaking, you commonly don't have the money to go out and reshoot a scene if it does not come out as you had planned. On multi-million dollar films, (and as an actor I've worked on several of them), the filmmakers can go back to the location; they can bring back the entire cast and crew, and re-film scenes if they don't like the way they turned out. In fact, I have been in movies where million dollar scenes were completely cut out of the final film. But, on the independent level, you really can't do that. So, what you want to do is to be as free, as spontaneous, as creative, and as in-the-moment as possible. From this, you allow yourself to take advantage of whatever is happening. If you see a location, go film there. If the sun is setting and the light's getting low; okay, you add that to your movie. If the sun's coming up or if it's a bright sunny day or if it starts to rain, add all that to the story development of your film.

From shooting a film in this fashion you add to the overall production value and presentation of your movie. Plus, you present your audience with additional depth to your stories and your character's development.

There are three man points to remember in Zen Filmmaking:

1. Don't lock yourself into a script
2. Don't lock yourself into locations.

3. Bring a cast and a crew on board who get the idea of, *"Spontaneous Creativity."*

    From this, everything becomes free. It becomes easy. It becomes, for lack of a better term, *"A spiritual process of filmmaking."*

    Like I always say, *"Zen Filmmaking leads to Cinematic Enlightenment."* What does that mean? It means by being free, by allowing the natural flow of creativity to guide you and your process, your film become as natural, as free, and as spiritual as possible. And from that, true art can be lived and created.

FADE OUT.

THE ZEN

Notes:

www.ingramcontent.com/pod-product-compliance
Lightning Source LLC
Chambersburg PA
CBHW071458070426
42452CB00040B/1886